METASTATIC CANCER CHEMISTRY

By

Dr. Vinod Jena

Assistant Professor
Department of Chemistry
(Government College Sarona Kanker CG India)

&

Dr. Natalija Matic

Research Scientist
(Hrvatske Vode, Zagreb, Croatia)

LP Inc. Publisher North Carolina USA

January 2016

Although great care has not been taken to provide accurate and current information, neither the author nor the publisher, nor anyone else associated with this publication, shall be liable for any loss, damage, or liability directly or indirectly caused or alleged to be caused by this book. The material contained herein is not intended to provide specific advice or recommendations for any specific situation

First Printing: 2016

ISBN: 978-1-329-84201-4

DEDICATION

To our friends all over the world.

Thank you all.

Without your support and patience,

we would have never achieved our dream.

ACKNOWLEDGMENTS

We would like to thank our teachers, friends all over the world
& especially editor, whose help this book would never have been completed.
Thank you for your patience and guidance

Preface to the First Edition

Cancer is an elusive, complex, and difficult disease to treat. Conventional treatments, such as chemotherapy, radiation, and surgery, are usually the only options initially offered to cancer patients, but they aren't always effective. Fortunately, integrative, naturopathic, and other types of "alternative" medicine frequently offer more effective solutions, which have been proven in clinical outcomes studies and in doctors' experiences with their patients.

In this book, various stages of metastasis & treatments of various types of cancers are described, all of which have effectively helped many cancer patients live long, productive lives. Also, the information found within this book is intended to provide an overview of metastatic cancer. I believe that readers will find that the book offers an informative and comprehensive overview of the metastatic cancer treatments available in integrative medicine.

Dr. V. Jena & Dr. N. Matic

(Author)

CONTENTS

What is Cancer?

Cancer can be defined as a disease in which a group of abnormal cells grow uncontrollably by disregarding the normal rules of cell division. These cells divide and produce new cells in an uncontrolled way that can spread throughout the body and cause damage to essential organs.

Normal cells are constantly subject to signals that dictate whether the cell should divide, differentiate into another cell or die. Cancer cells develop a degree of autonomy from these signals, resulting in uncontrolled growth and proliferation. If this proliferation is allowed to continue and spread, it can be fatal. In fact, almost 90% of cancer-related deaths are due to tumour spreading a process called metastasis. When cancer spreads to other parts of the body, this is called metastasis. Metastases can occur when cancer cells enter the bloodstream or lymph system. These systems circulate all over the body and allow the cells to travel. Tumors are masses (or lumps) that can develop as abnormal cells accumulate. Not all tumors are cancer . Benign (non-cancerous or nonmalignant) tumors do not spread to other parts of the body and are rarely life-threatening.

There are more than 125 different types of cancer. Most types of cancer lead to the formation of tumors, abnormal clusters of cells. However, not all tumors are cancerous. Tumors that cannot invade neighboring tissues or spread to other parts of the body are called benign tumors. With rare exceptions, benign tumors do not cause serious disease and are not life threatening. Malignant tumors are cancerous tumors. Malignant tumors can invade and destroy neighboring tissues and organs, and spread to other parts of the body. This spread of cancer cells from one part of the body to another distant site is called metastasis. In short, malignant tumors are capable of invasion and metastasis, but benign tumors do not have these capabilities.

Cancer Terms

Cancer has its own language that is unfamiliar to most people when they are newly diagnosed.

Here are keys to help you say the cancer terms used here. The words are in ABC order:

anesthesia = AN-es-THEE-zhuh

anesthesiologist = AN-es-THEE-zee-AHL-uh-jist

aspiration = ASP-er-AY-shun

autologous transfusion = aw-TAHL-uh-gus trans-FEW-zhun)

biopsy = BY-op-see

colonoscopy = KO-lun-AH-skuh-pee

colostomy = kuh-LAHS-tuh-mee

cryosurgery = CRY-o-SUR-juh-ree

curative = KUR-uh-tiv

cytoreductive = SY-toe-ree-DUK-tiv

endoscope = EN-doe-scope

endoscopy = en-DAHS-kuh-pee endotracheal = EN-doe-TRAKE-ee-ul

impotence = IM-puh-tense

incision = in-SIH-zhun

incisional biopsy = in-SIH-zhun-ul BY-op-see

incontinence = in-KON-tuh-nense

intraoperative = IN-truh-OP-er-ah-tiv

laparoscope = LAP-uh-ruh-scope

laparoscopic = LAP-uh-ruh-SKAH-pick

laparoscopy= LAP-uh-RAHS-kuh-pee

laparotomy = LAP-uh-ROT-uh-mee

mastectomy = mas-TEK-tuh-mee

mediastinoscopy = ME-dee-uh-stin-AH-skuh-pee

ostomy = OS-tuh-mee

palliative = PAL-ee-uh-tiv

photoablation = FOE-toe-uh-BLAY-shun

photocoagulation = FOE-toe-ko-ag-you-LAY-shun

pneumonia = new-MOAN-yuh

polyps = PAH-lips

prophylactic = PRO-fuh-LACK-tik

radical prostatectomy = RAD-ick-uhl PROS-tuh-TECK-tuh-mee

thoracoscope = thor-ACK-uh-scope

thoracoscopic = thor-ACK-uh-SKAH-pick

thoracoscopy = THOR-uh-KAH-skuh-pee

thoracotomy = THOR-uh-KOT-uh-mee

Metastatic Cancer

Metastatic cancer is a cancer that has spread from the part of the body where it started (the primary site) to other parts of the body. When cancer cells break away from a tumor, they can travel to other areas of the body through the bloodstream or the lymph system (which contains a collection of vessels that carry fluid and immune system cells). Metastatic tumours always start from cancer cells in another part of the body. For example, breast cancer can spread from its primary site (the breast) to form a new tumour in a different part of the body, such as the bones. The cancer cells in this second tumour are the same as the cells in the primary tumour – they are breast cancer cells, and not bone cancer cells. When this happens, it is called metastatic breast cancer, and not bone cancer.

Metastatic cancer may also be called:

- a secondary tumour or cancer

- metastasis (singular)

- metastases (plural)

This image(Figure 1) shows some parts of the lymph system, like lymph nodes and lymph vessels, as well as organs and tissues that contain many lymphocytes (immune cells)

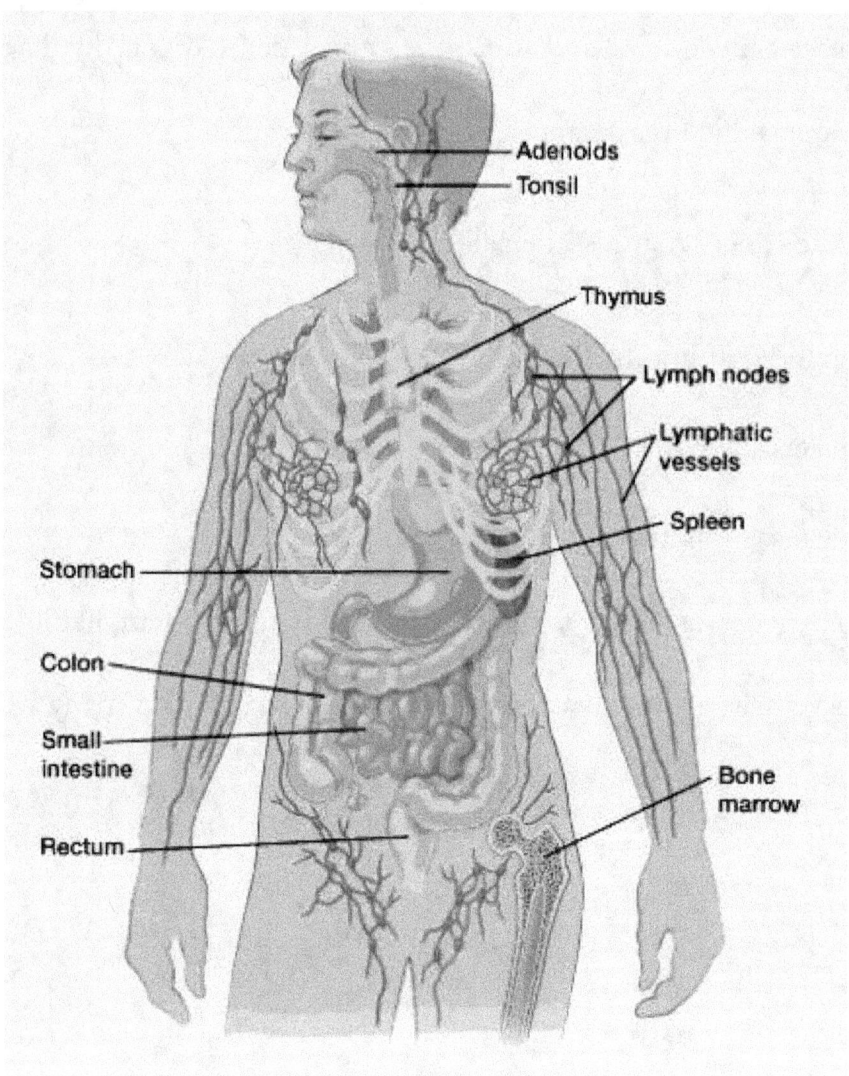

Figure 1: Lymph System

If the cells travel through the lymph system, they may end up in nearby lymph nodes (small, bean-sized collections of immune cells) or they may spread to other organs. More often, cancer cells that break off from the main tumor travel through the bloodstream. Once in the blood, they can go to any part of the body. Many of these cells die, but some may settle in a new area, begin to grow, and form new tumors. This spread of cancer to a new part of the body is called metastasis.

Cancer cells have to go through several steps to spread to new parts of the body:.

- They have to be able to break away from the original tumor and enter the bloodstream or lymph system, which can carry them to another part of the body.

- They need to attach to the wall of a blood or lymph vessel and move through it into a new organ.

- They need to be able to grow and thrive in their new location.

- They need to be able to avoid attacks from the body's immune system.

  Going through all these steps means the cells that start new tumors may no longer be exactly the same as the ones in the tumor they started in. This may make them harder to treat.

Even when cancer has spread to a new area, it's still named after the part of the body where it started. Treatment is also based on where the cancer started. For example, if prostate cancer spreads to the bones, it's still prostate cancer (not bone cancer), and the doctor will recommend treatments that have been shown to help against metastatic prostate cancer. Likewise, breast cancer that has spread to the lungs is still breast cancer, not lung cancer, and is treated as metastatic breast cancer.

Sometimes the metastatic tumors have already begun to grow when the cancer is first found and diagnosed. And in some cases, a metastasis may be found before the original (primary) tumor is found. If a cancer has already spread to many places when it's found, it may be very hard to figure out where it started

Stages of Metastasis

Metastasis occurs when cancer cells break away from the original tumor. The cells travel through the body via the blood or lymphatic system to another part of the body where they grow and proliferate forming a new tumor (Figure 2).

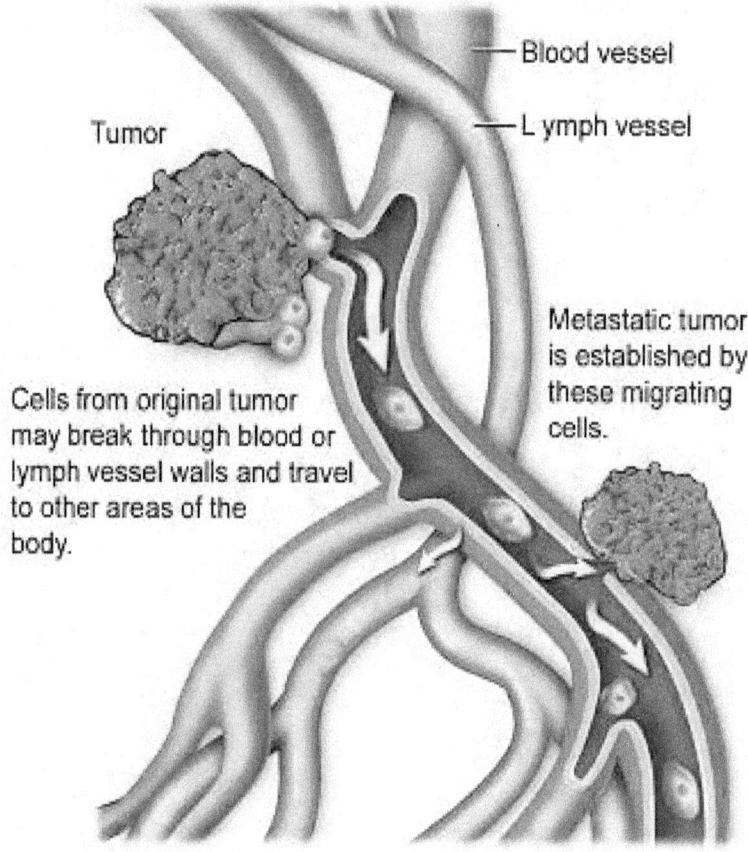

Blood vessel

Lymph vessel

Tumor

Metastatic tumor
is established by
these migrating
cells.

Cells from original tumor
may break through blood or
lymph vessel walls and travel
to other areas of the
body.

Figure 2 : The Metastatic Process

Cancers are named according to the tissue from which they originate.

When cancer cells metastasize and a new tumor grows in a different tissue,

it is still the same cancer. For example, lung cancer often metastasizes and causes tumors in the brain, bones, and liver Therefore, someone with lung cancer may have tumors in several different places, but all of the tumors are the result of the lung cancer, which has metastasized to other locations.

The migration of cancer cells from the primary location to a distant site is a complex biological process that involves changes at the molecular, cellular and physical level.

1. Local invasion: In this process, the small in situ tumour breaks through the basement membrane barrier

2. Intravasation: The tumour cells move through the walls of the capillaries or lymphatics into the circulatory system. This is a critical step in this pathway and it involves a complex, morphological change, wherein the cancer cell acquires properties of invasiveness and cell motility. This enables the cancer cell to push its way through the capillary wall and into the circulatory system.

3. Transport: Cancer cells travel through the blood or lymph until they anchor to a solid supporting tissue. Although both blood and lymph are responsible for transport, most of the distant metastases are caused by circulation through the bloodstream. At this stage, most of the cancer cells can be lost or destroyed due to hostile conditions. However, surviving cancer cells get lodged in the first set of capillaries they encounter (mainly due the large cells blocking the small passage of the capillaries) and form microthrombi.

4. Extravasation: This final step of migration is essentially similar to intravasation, in which eventually move into the tissues they are lodged in, typically lungs, brain or liver. The main difference is that the direction of movement is reversed. Cancer cells in the microthrombi now push through the capillary wall and into the tissue microenvironment.

5. Formation of micrometastasis: Upon extravasation, the cancer cells are now able to reactivate the cell proliferation pathways and form a small

tumour mass which either develops in the lumen of the capillary or through the vessel wall.

6. Colonization: This is the most complex and challenging stage mainly because the new environment may not always provide the necessary survival and proliferation factors needed for growth. Most cancer cells usually die or survive for long periods as micrometastases.

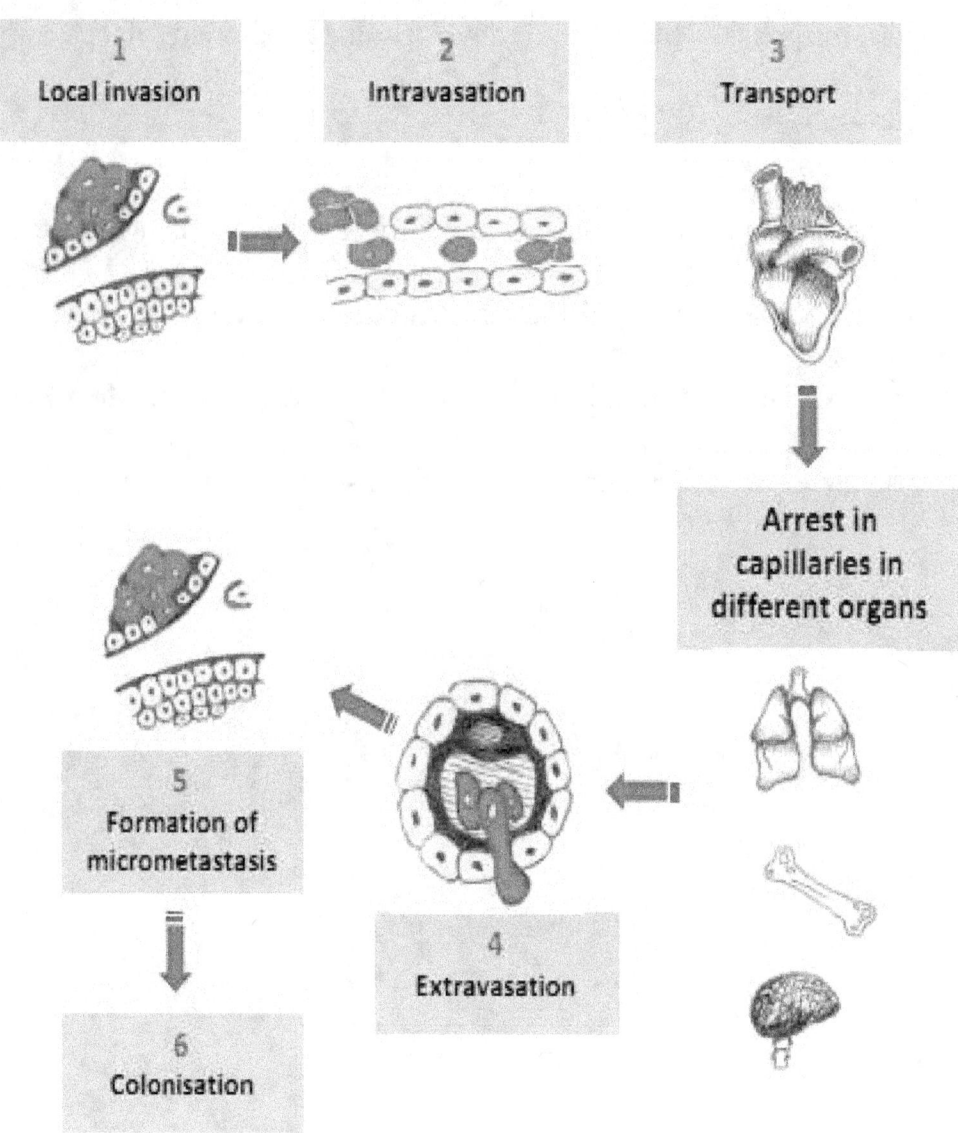

Figure 3: Biological pathways of cancer metastasis

However, the completion of all of the 6 steps outlined above does not always occur and the process of metastasis is highly inefficient, with colonization being the least efficient. In order for the tumour cell to become metastatic, several changes are needed to allow intra and extra-vasation as well as colonization. The complexity of this process is exemplified by carcinoma cells in particular. These cancer cells activate a cell differentiation circuit called EMT (Epithelial to Mesenchymal Transition) by inducing expression of several EMT-permissive transcription factors. This allows the cancer cell to acquire characteristics of mesenchymal cells such as invasiveness and motility.

These changes in characteristics involves several proteins responsible for tissue invasion and spread, and some of the key points are outlined below

(i)   One of the most important proteins is the cell-cell adhesion molecules (CAMs), whose main role is to tether cells to surrounding tissue. Among the CAMs, the most common protein implicated in metastasis is E-cadherin, found in all epithelial cells. In normal cells, E-cadherin acts as a bridge between adjacent cells, enabling cytoplasmic contact and sharing intracellular signaling factors responsible for inhibiting invasion and metastatic capability. Most epithelial cancers show a loss of E-cadherin function and this elimination plays a significant role in metastatic capability.

(ii) Another class of proteins involved in tissue invasion are the integrins, a widely distributed family of heterodimeric transmembrane adhesion receptors, which link cells to the extracellular matrix. In addition to their role in angiogenesis, they also play a central role in cell adhesion and migration, control of cell differentiation, proliferation and survival. Changes in integrin expression are also evident in invasive and metastatic cells. Successful colonization of new sites (both local and distant) demands adaptation, which is achieved by changing integrin subunits displayed by the migrating cells. For example, carcinoma cells facilitate invasion by preferentially expressing integrin subunits needed for binding to degraded stromal components by extracellular proteases.

(iii) Another strategy in successful colonization is increasing expression of extracellular proteases (such as MMPs – Matrix MetalloProteinases) while decreasing levels of protease inhibitors. Cells in the stroma close to cancer cells secrete active proteases, which facilitate invasion by degrading components of the extracellular matrix. This enables cancer cells to migrate across blood vessel boundaries and through normal epithelial cell layers.

All the proteins listed above are vital for invasion and metastatic ability. However, the regulatory and molecular circuits seem to differ in various tissue environments and their precise roles in different types of tumours are highly variable. Invasion and metastasis represents the last great frontier for exploratory cancer research. The challenge is to apply the new molecular insights about tissue invasiveness and metastasis to the development of effective therapeutic strategies.

Why is metastasis dangerous?

Metastasis is of great importance since most of the cancer deaths are caused by spread of the primary cancer to distant sites. In most cases, cancer patients with localized tumors have a better chance at survival than those with metastatic tumors.

New evidence shows that 60% to 70% of patients have initiated the metastatic process by the time of diagnosis. In addition, even patients that have no evidence of tumor spread at diagnosis are at risk for metastatic disease and need to be treated accordingly.

How cancer spreads?

As cancer cells divide, they can invade and grow directly into surrounding tissue or structures (direct extension). But, they can also break off from the original (primary) tumour and enter the bloodstream or lymphatic system. If the cancer cells are not detected by the immune system, which helps defend the body against infection and disease, they can be carried by the blood and lymph to form a new tumour in another area of the body. A tumour in a new location must develop its own blood supply (a process called angiogenesis) to survive and grow.

Because blood cells travel throughout the body, blood-related cancers like leukemia, lymphoma and multiple myeloma are usually not localizedlocalizedConfined or restricted to the original (primary) site with no evidence of spread. when the cancer is diagnosed. These cancer cells may be found in the blood, lymph nodes or other parts of the body, such as the liver or bones. This type of spread is not typically called a metastasis.

Why cancer cells tend to spread to certain parts of the body

Where a cancer starts often plays a role in where it will spread. Most cancer cells that break free from the original tumor are carried in the blood or lymph until they get trapped in the next "downstream" organ or set of lymph nodes. Once the cells are there, they can start new tumors. This explains why breast cancer often spreads to underarm lymph nodes, but rarely to lymph nodes in the groin. Likewise, there are many cancers that commonly spread to the lungs. This is because the heart pumps blood from the rest of the body through the lungs' blood vessels before sending it elsewhere. The liver is a common site of spread for cancer cells that start in the colon because blood from the intestines flows into the liver.

Cancer cells often break away from the main (primary) tumor and travel through the blood and/or lymph system, but they don't always settle in and start new tumors. Most of the time, the cells that broke away die. When cancer does spread to other organs and start to form new tumors, it's because of certain genetic changes in the cells that scientists are now starting to understand. Someday, doctors may be able to tell if a person's cancer is the type that will spread to other organs by looking for these genetic changes. Research is also focusing on treatments that block or target these genetic changes so the cancer cells can't spread and grow.

Sometimes the patterns of spread cannot be explained by where things are in the body. Some cancer cells are able to find and invade certain sites far away from where they started. For example, advanced prostate cancer often moves into the bones before spreading to other organs. This "homing" pattern may be caused by substances on the cancer cell surfaces that stick to cells in certain organs.

Why cancers spread?

All cancers have the potential to spread. Whether metastases will develop depends on many factors:

- **The type of cancer**

- Some types of cancer tend to spread to certain parts of the body.

- Breast cancer most often spreads to the bones, liver, lung or brain.

- Colorectal cancer tends to spread to the liver.

- Lung cancer often spreads to the brain, bones or liver.

- Prostate cancer tends to spread to the bones.

The grade of the cancer

- Low-grade cancer cells are less aggressive and are less likely to metastasize.

- High-grade cancer cells are more aggressive and are more likely to metastasize.

The length of time the cancer has been present

- The risk of metastasis increases the longer a tumour is in the body.

The cancer cells' ability to create a blood supply in a new location

- A cancerous tumour needs to set up a blood supply to grow.

The location of the primary tumour

Each type of cancer has a particular way that it spreads. Many metastases develop in the first area of blood vessels that cancer cells come to after leaving the primary tumour. After leaving the primary tumour, the lungs are one of the first places metastatic cells can be carried to by the bloodstream. This may explain why metastases form in the lungs.

Which cancers spread where?

This is a brief description of where certain cancers are most likely to spread. It's not a list of every place where a cancer could spread. For more details on these cancers, see our information on the specific cancer site.

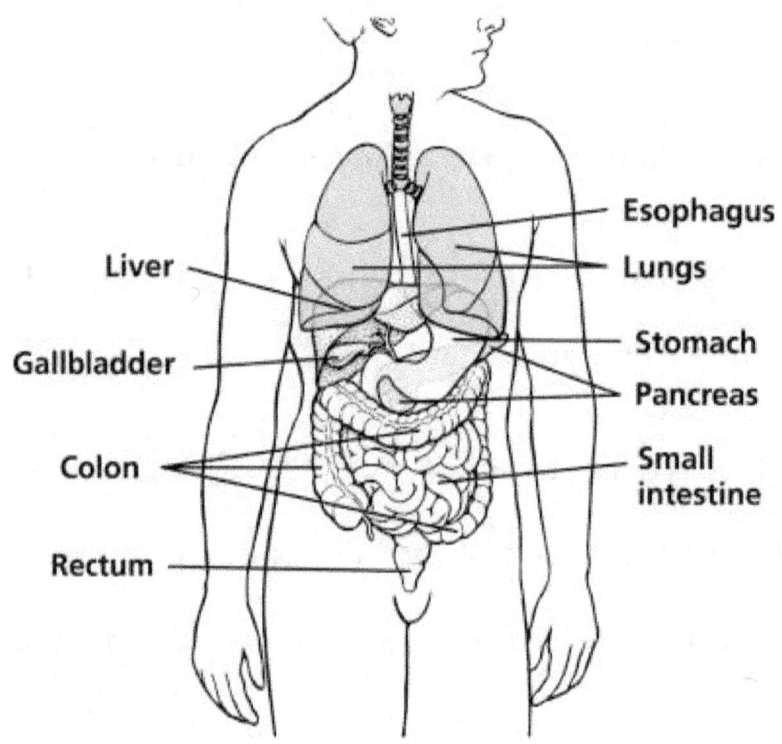

Bladder

Bladder cancer tends to stay in the same area (the pelvis) and grow into nearby tissues such as the pelvic wall. It can also spread to the lungs, liver, and bone.

Brain

Brain tumors rarely spread outside the brain. They mainly grow within the brain and sometimes into the spinal cord.

Breast

Breast cancer most commonly spreads to the bones, but also can spread to the liver, lungs, and brain. As the cancer progresses, it may affect any organ. It can also spread to the skin of the chest (near where the cancer started).

Cervix

Cancer of the cervix tends to grow near where it started, into the vagina and uterus and then other parts of the pelvis, such as the rectum and bladder. It can also grow into the bones and nerves of the spine, and spread to the liver, lungs, and bones.

Colon and rectum

The most common sites for colon or rectal cancer spread are the liver and lungs. These cancers may also spread to nearly any other organ, including the bones and brain.

Rectal cancer can also spread within in the pelvis, where the cancer started. This can be painful because it often grows into nerves and bones in this area.

Esophagus

Esophageal cancer mostly grows near where it started (in the chest and belly). As it progresses, it may grow into nearby organs or major blood vessels, which can make it hard to treat.

Kidney

Kidney (renal) cancer can grow where it started and invade nearby tissues. It can grow from the kidney into the large vein that drains the blood from the kidney (the renal vein). From there it can grow into a large vein that empties into the heart (the inferior vena cava). It can also grow from the kidney into the adrenal gland, which sits on top of the kidney. When it spreads, the lungs and bones are the most common sites.

Leukemia

Because they are already in the blood, leukemias can be considered to have spread throughout the body when they are diagnosed. They can progress by filling the bone marrow with leukemia cells. The normal bone marrow is replaced and cannot make new blood cells.

Some leukemias may spread outside the blood and into the fluid that surrounds the brain and spinal cord. Tumors made up of leukemia cells can also occur in the skin or in other parts of the body, but this is not common. In some types of leukemia, the cancer cells collect in the spleen, causing it to become large. Less often, leukemia cells settle in the liver, causing it to enlarge. In one type of leukemia, the cells deposit in the gums, so that they become red and swollen.

Liver

Liver cancer doesn't often spread outside the liver. It tends to grow throughout the liver as it becomes advanced. If it does spread, it's most often to the lungs or bones.

Lung

Lung cancer can spread to almost any organ of the body, but most often it will spread to the adrenal glands, liver, bones, or brain. It can also spread to the other lung.

Lymphoma

Lymphoma can affect any part of the body. While most start in the lymph nodes, spleen, and/or bone marrow, some start in lymph tissue in the stomach, intestines, or even the eye socket. Lymphomas can spread within the lymph system to distant parts of the body. Less often, they spread outside the lymph system to other organs, such as the lungs, liver, or bone. Lymphomas can affect the brain and spinal cord, either initially (called primary central nervous system lymphoma) or as spread to the fluid and tissues (the meninges) surrounding the brain and spinal cord. This is called lymphomatous meningitis.

Melanoma

Melanoma can spread anywhere in the body. It first tends to go to lymph nodes near where it started, but then can spread to the brain, lungs, liver, and bones. It can also spread to other areas of skin.

Mouth and throat

Cancers of the mouth, throat, or nasal passages tend to stay in the same area. When they spread, it's usually to the lungs. Less often they may spread to the liver or bones.

Multiple myeloma

Multiple myeloma can cause tumors called plasmacytomas. These tumors can spread to the bones anywhere in the body, but they rarely spread to other organs.

Ovary

Ovarian cancer most often spreads to the lining of the abdomen (belly) and pelvis (this lining is called theperitoneum), the omentum (a layer of connective tissue that drapes the abdominal cavity like an apron), and organs in the pelvis and belly. It can cause a build-up of fluid and swelling in the abdomen. It can also spread to the outer lining of the lungs and cause fluid to build up there. As it becomes more advanced, it may spread to the lung and liver, or, rarely, to the brain or skin.

Pancreas

Pancreatic cancer mainly stays in the abdomen (belly). It tends to grow into nearby tissues and may spread to the liver or other nearby organs. It can also spread to the lungs.

Prostate

Advanced prostate cancer most often goes to the bones. Much less often, it will spread to other organs, including the lungs and liver.

Stomach

Stomach (gastric) cancer tends to spread to nearby tissues and stay within the abdomen (belly). It may also spread to the liver or distant lymph nodes. Spread to the lungs, bones, and brain is less common.

Uterus

Cancer that starts in the uterus can grow into the vagina as well as nearby tissues in the pelvis. It also commonly spreads to the peritoneum (the lining of the abdominal cavity and pelvis) and the omentum (a layer of connective tissue that drapes the abdominal cavity like an apron). Other sites of cancer spread include the liver, lungs, and, less often, bones.

Metastasis "seed and soil theory" and organs susceptible

Metastasis is one of three hallmarks of malignancy or cancer as opposed to a benign tumor. Most tumors and other neoplasms can metastasize. The degree of ability to spread, however, varies between different types of tumors. For example, basal cell carcinoma rarely spreads. Some organs are more prone than others to metastasis of primary tumors. This was first discussed as the "seed and soil" theory by Stephen Paget over a century ago in 1889. For example, bones are the favoured site for prostate cancer, colon cancer spreads to liver, stomach cancer can metastasize to the ovaries and is then called Krukenberg tumor. The theory states that cancer cells find survival outside their primary suites difficult. To spread they need to find a location with similar characteristics. For example, breast cancer cells need calcium ions from breast milk to proliferate. Thus they may prefer the bones as a site of spread as bones are rich in calcium. Malignant melanoma favors melanocytes and nerves and thus may spread to the brain since the neural tissue and melanocytes arise from the same cell line in the embryo.

Challenges to the "seed and soil" theory

This "seed and soil" theory was challenged by James Ewing in 1928 who suggested that metastasis occurs purely by anatomic and mechanical routes. He suggested the spread via lymphatic channels and blood vessels. He noted that cancer cells affected the regional lymph nodes near the primary tumor. This is called nodal involvement, positive nodes, or regional disease. Primary tumors need biopsies of at least two lymph nodes near a tumor site when doing surgery to examine or remove a tumor. Localized spread to regional lymph nodes near the primary tumor is not normally counted as metastasis, although this is a sign of poor outcome.

Bone Cancer Metastasis

Metastasis can occur when cancer cells break away from the primary tumor, where the cancer began. The cells may then enter the bloodstream or lymph system and travel to the bone marrow. "The matrix of the bone marrow secretes cytokines," Fasano says. These proteins may attract cancer cells.

Cancer cells can remain hidden and inactive in bone for a long time. This means they can evade treatment. At some point, however, the cells may begin to multiply and grow new blood vessels to obtain oxygen and food. This allows a tumor or tumors to form.

Signs and Symptoms of Bone Metastasis

Bone metastasis can cause major pain. For example, a metastasis in the hipbone might be more painful than one in a rib bone.

At first, it may be hard to tell what's causing your symptoms. "And it may be hard to remember that not all pain is caused by the cancer," Fasano says. So it's important to tell your doctor right away if you have any of these symptoms of bone metastasis:

- Bone pain. This is often the first symptom of bone mets. It may come and go at first. It is often worse at night and gets better with movement. However, over time, the pain doesn't go away.

- Broken bones. This occurs because bone metastases weaken bone and puts you at risk for fracture. Breaks are most common in the leg, arm, or a bone in the spine.

- Numbness, paralysis, or trouble urinating. Pressure on the spinal cord from bone metastases in the spine can cause this.

- Loss of appetite, nausea, extreme thirst, confusion, or tiredness.These symptoms may be due to high levels of calcium in the blood. As metastasis develops in the bone, there is release of calcium into the bloodstream.

Metastasis in the bone may cause:

- Severe, progressive pain

- Swelling

- Bones that are more easily fractured or broken

Types of Treatment for Bone Metastasis

How doctors treat bone metastasis depends on the extent and location of the bony lesion. Treatments include:

- Treating the underlying cancer. This is the most important step, Fasano tells WebMD. Treatment depends on the type of tumor and where it started in your body. Treatment often includes a combination of drugs that were used to treat the primary cancer when you were first diagnosed.

- Bisphosphonates. Bisphosphonate drugs such as Aredia and Zometa help prevent the breakdown of bone, which can ease pain and reduce your risk of fractures. Bisphosphonate therapy is especially important if the metastasis is in a weight-bearing bone or is causing a great deal of pain. If metastasis in the spine is causing severe pain and risking a collapse of vertebrae, Fasano sends the patient for an orthopedic evaluation. For elevatedcalcium levels, patients will often need intravenous fluids, bisphosphonates, and other medications to help lower levels.

- Denosumab (Xgeva). Denosumab is injected under the skin, rather than by infusion, and also helps prevent bone breakdown. It's more expensive than bisphosphonates, so some insurance companies will pay for it only after you've first tried a bisphosphonate.

- Vertebroplasty. In this outpatient procedure, bone cement is injected into a fractured vertebra. The cement hardens quickly and can dramatically improve back pain within hours.

- Surgery and/or radiation. If a fracture seems likely in the near future, an orthopaedic surgeon may insert a rod or pin to stabilize the bone. Radiation aims high-energy X-rays at the tumor to kill the cancer. If surgery isn't needed,radiation therapy alone may ease pain.

Treatment for bone metastasis can prolong life and relieve symptoms. Much depends upon the type of cancer you have, how old you are, and how much time has elapsed since you first were diagnosed.

Brain Cancer Metastasis

Brain metastasis is cancer that started in another part of the body and spread to the brain. It's sometimes called secondary brain cancer or a metastatic brain tumour. Brain metastasis is not the same as cancer that starts in the brain (called primary brain cancer). Brain metastases are much more common than primary brain cancer.

Terminology

The term brain technically includes the cerebrum, the cerebellum and the brainstem. As the cerebrum corresponds to the great majority of the brain volume and thus receives most of its blood supply, it is more common to metastatic lesions appear in the cerebral parenchyma. Consequently, the expression "cerebral metastases" is used as a synonym to "brain metastases".

Symptoms

The symptoms of brain metastases vary depending on which part of the brain is affected. The most common symptom of brain metastasis is headache. Headaches may be caused by a tumour pressing on the brain, swelling (called edema**edema** Swelling caused by an abnormal buildup of fluid in the body.), bleeding or hydrocephalus.

Other signs and symptoms of brain metastases include:

- nausea and vomiting

- seizure

- weakness or numbness in parts of the body, such as the face, arms or legs

- problems with memory and confusion

- changes in behaviour and personality

- problems with balance and coordination

- loss of bladder or bowel control (called incontinence)

- problems with speech

- problems with swallowing

Radiological Diagnosis

Brain metastasis can be diagnosed utilizing the following tests:

- Computed Axial Tomography (CAT Scan/CT) can be done with or without intravenous contrast and includes many different views of the brain. CTs are frequently the initial diagnostic test utilized.

- Magnetic Resonance Imaging (MRI) makes a clear picture of the brain using powerful magnets and radio waves. With the addition of an intravenous contrast agent, this is the gold standard in testing that provides information about the location, size, characteristics and pressure effects of the tumor.

- If a metastatic tumor is suspected, the treating neuro-oncologist or neurosurgeon may ask for further testing. Additional imaging of the body may be requested and is obtained generally in the form of a CT with contrast of the chest, abdomen and pelvis and a bone scan. These tests allow detection of a primary neoplasm elsewhere in the body. Additional testing may be indicated at times, but this constitutes the basic palette of tests.

Treatment Options

Symptom Management

The danger of brain metastases is the space they take up in the brain and the pressure they put on surrounding tissue. This pressure can cause the symptoms associated with brain lesions, such as headaches, speech difficulties, seizures, nausea/vomiting, weakness of a limb, or visual disturbances. The goal of initial therapy is to relieve some of this pressure on the brain tissue by decreasing swelling using medications called corticosteroids (dexamethasone, prednisone), either orally or through an intravenous (IV) line. Some patients may see relief of symptoms quickly after starting steroids, however this does not mean the tumor is gone. If patients experience seizures as a result of their brain metastases, they may also receive anti-seizure medications to prevent further seizures.

Treatment decisions for each patient are based on several factors, including tumor type, general health, age, presence/control of cancer outside of the brain, and number of brain metastases.

Surgery

For patients with a single brain lesion, surgery may be a good option, especially if the tumor is under control in the rest of the body. However, the lesion must be in an area of the brain where it is safe to operate. A study of patients with a single brain metastasis randomized to whole brain radiation therapy (WBRT) alone vs. surgery followed by WBRT found that patients treated with surgery and WBRT have fewer recurrences, and better quality of life than patients treated with WBRT alone. Life expectancy in these patients has also been shown to increase. However, these results do not apply to patients with radiosensitive tumors such as lymphomas, small cell lung cancer, and germ cell tumors.

Whole Brain Radiation Therapy

Whole brain radiotherapy (WBRT) is just what it sounds like – giving radiation to the entire brain. This is generally given in 10 to 15 doses (also called fractions), and is often used in patients with poor prognostic factors, patients who are not candidates for surgery, or patients with more than 3 brain lesions. Many patients may receive WBRT in combination with another therapy (surgery, radiosurgery). The motivation of treating the whole brain is that there may be cancer cells in the normal-appearing brain, but just not enough of them yet to form a mass and be seen by radiology studies. Thus, treatment of the whole brain attempts to kill all the cancer cells.

WBRT has been reported to improve symptoms of brain metastases in 70-90% of patients, although some of this benefit is also a result of the corticosteroids. Despite this symptom improvement, recurrence is common, and control of brain metastases may only be achieved in half of the patients. Patients with tumors that are more sensitive to the effects of radiation fare better (lung and breast, for example) than those with relatively radioresistant tumors (melanoma and renal cancers).

It is difficult to evaluate the long-term effects of WBRT, given the small number of patients that survive long-term. These effects could include dementia and a decline in cognitive and physical functioning.

Stereotactic Radiosurgery (SRS)

Stereotactic radiosurgery (SRS) is a confusing term. It is actually not surgery at all, but a highly precise administration of a large dose of radiation to the tumor site. Unlike traditional external beam radiation, which is usually given daily over many weeks, SRS is administered in a single dose (Gamma Knife®) or up to five doses (Cyberknife®) and other linear accelerator-based treatments). More than one brain tumor can be treated during one session (for example, if a patient had 2 separate brain metastases, both could be treated on the same day). Treatments are administered by a traditional radiation machine called a linear accelerator, or a specialized machine such as Gamma Knife®, Cyberknife®, XKnife® and ExacTrac®. Gamma Knife® delivers several hundred beams of radiation from a cobalt source. To take you back to high school chemistry, cobalt is one of the elements in the periodic table. It is the radioactive source used in this technique. The radiation beams concentrate at the point where all the beams meet (see picture). The radiation beams travel through hundreds of holes in the helmet to converge on the tumor, allowing a high dose of radiation to be delivered to the tumor, while sparing the surrounding tissue from the high dose. SRS is highly dependent on accuracy, and requires that the patient's head be securely stabilized using a helmet (head frame), so there is no movement during the treatment. Finally, there is a size limit for Gamma Knife; the metastases should be 3 cm or smaller.

Chemotherapy

Currently, no systemic chemotherapy treatments have received FDA approval for the treatment of brain metastases from solid tumors. It is widely believed that most chemotherapy agents are not able to cross the blood brain barrier. In other words, they move through the blood stream, but cannot enter the brain. As a result, the brain is a safe haven for cancer cells that "escape" the chemo and make their way there. However there are exceptions. Researchers have found that brain metastases from tumor types that are particularly sensitive to chemotherapy (for example testicular cancer, lymphomas, and small cell lung cancer) are also sensitive to chemotherapy. Research has also demonstrated that in those who have not already received a large amount of chemotherapy may have a greater reduction in brain metastases with chemotherapy treatment. This leads researchers to believe that there is some penetration of the blood brain barrier by chemotherapy, just not always in effective amounts. One chemotherapy agent, temozolomide (Temodar®), is an oral medication that is capable of crossing the blood-brain barrier. This medication is used to treat primary brain tumors and metastatic melanoma lesions.

Preventing Brain Metastases with WBRT: Prophylactic Cranial Irradiation

Small cell lung cancer is associated with a very high risk for brain metastases; approximately 50% of patients develop lesions within two years of diagnosis. For this reason, researchers looked at utilizing whole brain radiation as a way to prevent future brain metastases from developing. When whole brain radiation is given as a preventive measure, it is also known by the name "prophylactic cranial irradiation" or "PCI." Studies of PCI have shown significant decreases in brain mets (from 55% to 19% at 2 years and from 56% to 35% at 3 years) and increases in overall survival. Some have suggested there may be long-term neurologic impairment from this treatment, but long-term neurotoxicity data is lacking. PCI is the standard of care for patients with limited-stage small cell lung cancer who have complete remission after local therapy. Studies are ongoing to assess any benefits of this practice in other tumor types.

XKnife® is a linear accelerator- based treatment. Like Gamma Knife, it requires a head frame, which will remain on the patient for the entire procedure, providing a reference for the location of the patient's anatomy.

Cyberknife® is a form of frameless SRS using a specialized miniature linear accelerator with a robotic arm. It gets around the issue of using a frame for immobilization by using a custom mask for each patient along with skull-based tracking, allowing the robot to follow a target. Cyberknife can accommodate lesions larger than 3 cm, and can also be used to treat other types of cancer outside the brain.

Liver Cancer Metastasis

Liver metastases are cancerous tumors that have spread to the liver from somewhere else in the body. Cancer that starts in the liver is called hepatocellular carcinoma.

Causes

Almost any cancer can spread to the liver. Cancers that can spread to the liver include:

- Breast cancer

- Colorectal cancer

- Esophageal cancer

- Lung cancer

- Melanoma

- Pancreatic cancer

- Stomach cancer

The risk of cancer spreading to the liver depends on the location (site) of the original cancer. A liver metastasis may be present when the original (primary) cancer is diagnosed. Or it may occur months or years after the primary tumor is removed.

Metastasis to the liver may cause:

- Jaundice

- Itchy skin or rash

- Abnormally high enzymes in the liver

- Abdominal pain, appetite loss, nausea, and vomiting

Symptoms

In some cases, there are no symptoms. When symptoms occur, they may include:

- Anorexia

- Confusion

- Fever, sweating

- Jaundice (yellowing of the skin and whites of the eyes)

- Nausea

- Pain, usually in the upper right part of the abdomen

- Weight loss

Treatment

Treatment depends on:

- The primary cancer site

- How many liver tumors you have

- Whether the cancer has spread to other organs

- Your overall health

Types of treatments that may be used are described below:-

Surgery

When the tumor is only in one or a few areas of the liver, the cancer may be removed with surgery.

Chemotherapy

When the cancer has spread to the liver and other organs, whole-body (systemic) chemotherapy is usually used. The type of chemotherapy used depends on the original type of cancer. When the cancer has only spread in the liver, systemic chemotherapy may still be used. Chemoembolization is a type of chemotherapy to one area. A thin tube called a catheter is inserted into an artery in the groin. The catheter is threaded into the artery in the liver. Cancer-killing medicine is sent through the catheter. Then another medicine is sent through the catheter to block blood flow to the part of the liver with the tumor. This "starves" the cancer cells.

OTHER TREATMENTS

- Alcohol (ethanol) injected into the liver tumor -- A needle is sent through the skin directly into the liver tumor. The alcohol kills cancer cells.

- Heat, using radio or microwave energy -- A large needle called a probe is placed into the center of the liver tumor. Energy is sent through thin wires called electrodes, which are attached to the probe. The cancer cells are heated and die. This method is called radiofrequency ablation when radio energy is used. It is called microwave ablation when microwave energy is used.

- Freezing, also called cryotherapy -- A probe is placed in contact with the tumor. A chemical is sent through the probe that causes ice crystals to form around the probe. The cancer cells are frozen and die.

- Radioactive beads -- These beads deliver radiation to kill the cancer cells and block the artery that goes to the tumor. This procedure is called radioembolization. It is done in much the same way as chemoembolization.

Lung Cancer Metastasis

Lung metastases are cancerous tumors that start somewhere else in the body and spread to the lungs. Metastatic lung cancer occurs when lung cancer cells break away from a tumor and travel to other parts of your body through the blood or lymph system. Lung cancer can be metastatic at the time of diagnosis or following treatment. Because symptoms do not develop when lung cancer is present, it is common for the cancer to metastasize before it is diagnosed. Even though the cancer may have formed a tumor in a new location in the body, it is still named after the part of the body where it started. For example, if lung cancer spreads to the brain, it is called metastatic lung cancer. The most common sites of metastases for lung cancer are the other lung, adrenal gland, bones, brain and liver. If you have been treated for lung cancer and now have cancer cells in any of these areas, it is most likely that the lung cancer has spread.

Metastatic lung cancer is not the same as recurrent lung cancer. Recurrent lung cancer is cancer that returns to the same part of the same lung after treatment, rather than traveling to other parts of the body. If cancer develops in the lung that wasn't previously affected, it is almost always a new metastasized cancer, not a recurrence. In all cases, a metastatic tumor is always caused by cancer cells migrating from another part of the body.

Metastasis to the lungs may cause:

- Chronic cough or inability to get a full breath

- Abnormal chest X-ray

- Chest pain

- Other nonspecific systemic symptoms of metastatic breast cancer can include fatigue, weight loss, and poor appetite, but it's important to remember these can also be caused by medication or depression.

Lung cancer symptoms

 Early symptoms and signs of lung cancer

There may be no symptoms at the onset of the disease. When present, common symptoms of lung cancer may include:

- Coughing: This includes a persistent cough that doesn't go away or changes to a chronic "smoker's cough," such as more coughing or pain.

- Coughing up blood: Coughing up blood or rust-colored sputum (spit or phlegm) should always be discussed with your doctor.

- Breathing difficulties: Shortness of breath, wheezing or noisy breathing (called stridor) may all be signs of lung cancer.

- Loss of appetite: Many cancers cause changes in appetite, which may lead to unintended weight loss.

- Fatigue: It is common to feel weak or excessively tired.

- Recurring infections: Recurring infections, like bronchitis or pneumonia, may be one of the signs of lung cancer.

Signs of advanced stages of lung cancer

Advanced stages of lung cancer are often characterized by the spread of the cancer to distant sites in the body. This may affect the bones, liver or brain. As other parts of the body are affected, new lung cancer symptoms may develop, including:

- Bone pain

- Swelling of the face, arms or neck

- Headaches, dizziness or limbs that become weak or numb

- Jaundice

- Lumps in the neck or collar bone region

Treatment

Chemotherapy is usually used to treat metastatic cancer to the lung. Surgery to remove the tumors may be done when any of the following occurs:

- The first (primary) tumor has been removed

- The cancer has spread to only limited areas of the lung

- The lung tumors can be completely removed with surgery

However, the main tumor must be curable, and the patient must be strong enough to go through the surgery and recovery.

Kidney Cancer Metastasis

Renal cell carcinoma, also called kidney cancer, occurs when cancer cells form in the tubules of the kidney. Tubules are tiny tubes in the kidney that help filter waste products from the blood in order to make urine.

How the Cancer Spreads

Renal cell carcinoma can spread from a mass of cancer cells or tumor to other parts of the body in one of three ways:

- More cancer cells grow in the tissue around the tumor.

- The cancer moves into the lymph system, which has vessels throughout the body.

- Kidney cancer cells enter the bloodstream and are carried and deposited to another organ or location in the body.

Symptoms of Metastatic Renal Cell Carcinoma

When renal cell carcinoma is in its early stages, it's unlikely that you'll experience obvious symptoms. Noticeable symptoms are often a sign that the disease has metastasized.

Symptoms typically include:

- blood in the urine

- pain on one side of the lower back

- lump in the back or side

- weight loss

- fatigue

- fever

The Stages of Kidney Cancer

Renal cell carcinoma is classified in one of four stages:

- stages 1 and 2: cancer is present only in the kidney

- stage 3: the cancer has spread to a lymph node near the kidney or in a main kidney blood vessel or fatty tissue around the kidney

- stage 4: the cancer has spread to another organ or other lymph nodes or tissue

Metastatic Breast Cancer

Metastatic breast cancer occurs when breast cancer cells travel from the breast to another part of the body such as the bones, liver, lungs, or brain. Metastatic breast cancer is also referred to as Stage IV breast cancer. A second breast cancer that develops in the same or the other breast is not metastatic breast cancer. And having cancer cells in the lymph nodes does not mean your cancer is Stage IV, although pathologists sometimes use the term "metastatic to the lymph nodes."

What Are The Stages of Breast Cancer?

The five stages of breast cancer as follows:

Stage 0

In stage 0, the cancer is considered noninvasive. There are two types of stage 0 breast cancer:

- In ductal carcinoma in situ (DCIS), the cancer is found inside the lining of the milk ducts but hasn't spread to other breast tissue.

- Lobular carcinoma in situ (LCIS) is also a type of stage 0 breast cancer, but it isn't actually considered cancer. Instead, it describes abnormal cells that have formed in the lobules of the breast.

Stage 1

At this stage, the cancer is considered invasive but localized. It's highly treatable at this point. Stage 1 is divided into 1A and 1B forms:

- In stage 1A, the cancer is smaller than 2 centimeters. It hasn't spread to the surrounding lymph nodes.

- In stage 1B, your doctor might not find a tumor in your breast, but the lymph nodes may have tiny groupings of cancer cells. These groupings measure between 0.2 and 2 millimeters.

Both stages 0 and 1 are highly treatable.

Stage 2

The cancer is invasive in stage 2. It's still contained in the breast tissue. This stage is divided into 2A and 2B.

- In stage 2A, you may have no tumor, but the cancer has spread to your lymph nodes. Alternatively, the tumor might be less than 2 centimeters in size and involves the lymph nodes. Last, the tumor may measure between 2 and 5 centimeters but doesn't involve your lymph nodes.

- In stage 2B, the tumor size is larger. You may be diagnosed with 2B if your tumor is between 2 to 5 centimeters, and it has spread to four or fewer lymph nodes. Otherwise, the tumor might be bigger than 5 centimeters with no lymph node spread.

You may require stronger treatment than with the earlier stages. Still, the prognosis is still good at stage 2.

Stage 3

Cancer is considered invasive and advanced if it reaches stage 3. It hasn't yet spread to your organs. This stage is divided into the subsets 3A, 3B, and 3C.

- In stage 3A, your tumor may be smaller than 2 centimeters, but there are between four and nine affected lymph nodes. Tumor size at this stage may be larger than 5 centimeters and involve small gatherings of cells in your lymph nodes. The cancer may have also spread into the lymph nodes in your underarm and breastbone.

- In stage 3B, the tumor can be any size. At this point, it has also spread into your breastbone or skin and affects up to nine lymph nodes.

- In stage 3C, the cancer may have spread to over 10 lymph nodes even if no tumor is present. The lymph nodes affected may be near your collarbone, underarm, or breastbone.

Treatment options at stage 3 include:

- mastectomy

- radiation

- hormone therapy

- chemotherapy

These treatments are also offered in earlier stages. Your doctor may suggest a combination of treatments for the best outcome.

Stage 4

At stage 4, the breast cancer has metastasized. In other words, it has spread to other parts of the body. This can include one or more of the following:

- Brain

- Bones

- Lungs

- Liver

What causes metastatic breast cancer?

We still do not understand why some cancers become metastatic, especially those that are diagnosed years after the first breast cancer. In the past, doctors believed that cancer progressed in a linear manner and that women with positive lymph nodes were more likely to become metastatic. Now researchers are focusing more on genetics and the microbiology of breast cancer. They are trying to learn why some cancers behave more aggressively, what causes cancer cells to grow in different parts of the body, and what treatments can be developed to stop that process.

How Does Spreading Happen?

There are several ways cancer can spread in the body.

- Direct invasion happens when the tumor spread to a nearby organ in the body. The cancer cells take root and begin to grow in this new area.

- Lymphangitic spread has more to do with cancer traveling through the lymphatic system. Breast cancer often involves the nearby lymph nodes, so the cancer can enter the lymph circulatory system and take hold in different parts of the body.

- Hematogenous spread moves in much the same way as the lymphangitic spread but through the blood vessels. The cancer cells travel through the body and take root in remote areas and organs.

Where Can Breast Cancer Spread?

Breast cancer can spread to almost any area of the body. The most common regions that breast cancer may spread to in order of frequency are:

1. Bone

2. Lung

3. Liver

1. Bone: Approximately 25% of breast cancers spread first to the bone. The bones of the spine, ribs, pelvis, skull, and long bones of the arms and

legs are most often affected. There are two types of bone metastases: osteolytic and osteoblastic. With osteolytic metastases, the cancer eats away at the bone, forming holes. This most often occurs in the legs, hip, or pelvis. Osteoblastic metastases actually increasebone mineral density but also cause bones to fracture easily. Both types of bone metastases cause pain. Bone metastases can cause pain, decreased activity, and potentially severe problems such as fractures. Other complications that can arise from bone metastases include the surgical treatment for fractures, hypercalcemia (abnormally high levels of calcium), and spinal cord compression (vertebral damage due to pressure on the spinal cord).

Aredia is an FDA-approved drug used to treat some patients with advanced breast cancer. It is administered intravenously (through a vein) along with other cancer treatments, such as chemotherapy. Clinical studies have shown that breast cancer patients with bone metastases who are given Aredia tend to experience a delay in or reduction of bone pain, fractures, and other bone complications compared to patients who do not receive Aredia. Possible side effects of Aredia include fever, fatigue, nausea and vomiting, initial bone pain, lack of appetite, and anemia (decrease in red blood cells).

Other bisphosphonates have also shown promise in alleviating symptoms of bone metastases. In one study, a bisphosphonate called ibandronate stopped the progression of bone metastases in mice and halted the formation of new metastases. Other bisphosphonates in study include:

- Didronel (generic name, etidronate)

- Bonefos, Clostoban, Loron, Ostac (generic name, clodronate)

- Skelid (generic name, tiludronate)

- Fosamax (generic name, alendronate)

- Zometa (generic name, zoledronate)

At this time, most physicians do not see sufficient evidence to recommend bisphosphonates for breast cancer patients who do not already have bone metastases.

2. Lung: Between 60% and 70% of women who die from breast cancer have eventually had it spread to their lungs. In 21% of cases, the lung is the only site of metastatis (spread). The most common signs of lung metastases are: shortness of breath and dry cough. In some cases, women will not experience any symptoms; cancer will only be detected by chest X-ray or CT scan. In rare cases, part of the lung may be surgically removed if the cancer is confined to one area. However, in most cases, the cancer has spread itself throughout the lung and is more effectively treated bychemotherapy or other anti-cancer drugs.

3. Liver: The liver is the third most common site for breast cancer to spread to after bone and lung. Two-thirds of women with metastatic breast cancer eventually have it spread to the liver. Symptoms of liver

metastases are subtle at first but become increasing intense over time. Weight loss, loss of appetite, fever, and gastrointestinal disorders may indicate liver metastases. Liver blood tests may first detect cancer in the liver. However, a liver biopsy is necessary to distinguish between cancerous tumors and other abnormalities.

Breast cancer may also spread to other regions of the body. Though these sites are less common, breast cancer may infect the bone marrow, brain, ovaries, spinal cord, eye, and other areas.

How Is Metastasis Diagnosed?

A variety of tests can detect the spread of cancer. These tests typically aren't performed unless your doctor believes the cancer has spread. Before ordering them, your doctor will evaluate your tumor size, lymph node spread, and the specific symptoms you're having.

The most common tests include:

- a chest X-ray

- a bone scan

- a CT scan

- an MRI scan

- an ultrasound

- a positron emission tomography (PET) scan

How is Metastasis Treated?

Stage 4 breast cancer cannot be cured. Instead, once it's diagnosed, treatment is about extending and improving your quality of life.

The main forms of treatment for stage 4 breast cancer include:

- chemotherapy

- radiation therapy

- surgery

- hormone therapy

- targeted therapy

- clinical trials

- pain management

Metastatic Prostate Cancer

Metastatic prostate cancer occurs when cancer cells break away from the original tumor in your prostate gland. The cells spread to other parts of your body, traveling through your blood, lymphatic system, or tissue. Most often, prostate cancer spreads to the bones. It's also common for it to spread to the liver or lungs. It's rarer for it to spread to other organs, such as the brain. It's still prostate cancer, even when it spreads. For example, metastatic prostate cancer in a bone in your hip is not bone cancer. It has the same prostate cancer cells the original tumor had, and your treatment options are the same as when cancer was only in your prostate gland.

Metastatic prostate cancer is an advanced form of cancer. Although it can't be cured, it can be treated and controlled.

How Prostate Cancer Spreads

Metastasis happens when cancer cells break away from the original tumor and move to a blood or lymph vessel. Once there, they circulate through the body. The cells stop in capillaries - tiny blood vessels - at some distant location. The cells then break through the wall of the blood vessel and attach to whatever tissue they find. They multiply and grow new blood vessels to bring nutrients to the new tumor. Prostate cancer prefers to grow in specific areas, such as lymph nodes or in the ribs, pelvic bones, and spine. Most cancer cells that break away form new tumors. Many others don't survive in the bloodstream. Some die at the site of the new tissue. Others may lie inactive for years or never become active.

Chances of Developing Metastatic Prostate Cancer

About 50% of men diagnosed with local prostate cancer will develop metastatic cancer during their lifetime. Finding cancer early and treating it can lower that rate.

A small percentage of men aren't diagnosed with prostate cancer until it has become metastatic. Doctors can tell it's metastatic cancer by taking a small sample of the tissue and studying the cells.

Skin Metastasis

Skin, or cutaneous, metastasis (plural 'metastases') refers to growth of cancer cells in the skin originating from an internal cancer. In most cases, cutaneous metastasis develops after the initial diagnosis of the primary internal malignancy (e.g. breast cancer, lung cancer) and late in the course of the disease. In very rare cases, skin metastasis may occur at the same time or before the primary cancer has been discovered and may be the prompt for further thorough investigation.

Skin metastasis may also occur from a skin cancer, usually melanoma. The original or 'primary' melanoma produces metastases or 'secondary' growths in surrounding or distant skin sites and other tissues such as the lungs or brain.

What causes skin metastasis?

Skin metastasis occurs when cancerous cells break away from the primary tumour and make their way to the skin through the blood circulation or lymphatic system. Most malignant tumours can produce skin metastasis, but some are more likely to do so than others. When the following cancers have metastasised, they have quite a high chance of affecting the skin.

- Melanoma – 45% chance of developing skin metastasis (but only 15 to 20% of melanomas metastasise, so the overall chance of a skin metastasis is about 7-10%)

- Breast cancer – 30%

- Nasal sinus cancers – 20%

- Cancer of the larynx – 16%

- Cancer of the oral cavity – 12%

The incidence of skin metastasis varies but is somewhere between 3-10% in patients with a primary malignant tumour.

Signs and Symptoms of Skin Metastasis

Most skin metastasis occurs in a body region near the primary tumour. The first sign of skin metastasis is often the development of a firm, round or oval, mobile, non-painful nodule. The nodules are rubbery, firm or hard in texture and vary in size from barely noticeable lesions to large tumours. These may be skin coloured, red, or in the case of melanoma, blue or black. Sometimes multiple nodules appear rapidly. The skin metastases may break down and ulcerate through the skin. Specific patterns include:

- Carcinoma erysipeloides: sharply demarcated red patch due to local spread of primary cancer blocking lymphatic blood vessels in adjacent skin.

- En cuirasse or sclerodermoid carcinoma: indurated fibrous scar-like plaques due to cancer cells infiltrating collagen in the skin

- Carcinoma telangiectoides: red patches with numerous blood vessels (telngiectases) or lymphatic vessels (lymphangioma-like)

Depending on the location of the primary tumour, skin metastasis display certain characteristic features.

Organ of Cancer origin	Features of skin Metastasis
Breast	• Most common sites of skin metastasis are the chest and abdomen • Less common sites include scalp, neck, upper extremities and back • Some patients may develop a firm scar-like area in the skin. If this occurs on the scalp, hair may be lost (alopecia neoplastica) • Lesions may appear as inflammatory plaques with a clear cut raised margin (carcinoma erysipeloides)
Lung	• Most common sites are the chest, abdomen and back • Reddish firm nodules suddenly appear in the skin • Nodules tend to follow the intercostal vessels when they appear on the chest
Melanoma	• In men, skin metastasis occurs on the chest, extremities and back • In women, metastasis to the lower extremities is common
Colon and stomach	• Common sites are the abdomen and the pelvis • A nodule appearing at the umbilicus is a sign of extensive colorectal cancer

What is the treatment for skin metastasis?

The underlying primary tumour needs to be treated. However, in most cases where skin metastasis has occurred, the primary cancer is widespread and may be untreatable. In this case, palliative care is given and includes keeping lesions clean and dry. Debridement can be done if lesions bleed or crust. Other therapies that may be helpful include:

- Imiquimod cream – may lead to regression of metastasis in some cases of melanoma

- Liquid nitrogen cryotherapy

- Photodynamic therapy

- Excision

- Carbon dioxide laser therapy

- Pulsed dye laser therapy

- Intralesional chemotherapy and cytokines

- Electrochemotherapy, a new treatment that uses electrical impulses to enhance effectiveness bleomycin or cisplatin injected into tumours.

Colorectal Cancer

Colorectal cancer happens when cells that are not normal grow in your colon or rectum . These cells grow together and form polyps. Over time, some polyps can turn into cancer. This cancer is also called colon cancer or rectal cancer, depending on where the cancer is.

Symptoms of Metastatic Colorectal Cancer

Metastatic colorectal cancer symptoms depend on where the cancer has spread, as well as the size and location of the tumor within the body.

Patients with metastatic colorectal cancer will not always notice symptoms before a diagnosis.

- If the bones are affected, symptoms may include pain, fractures, constipation or decreased alertness due to high calcium levels.

- If the lungs are affected, symptoms may include shortness of breath or difficulty breathing, coughing, chest wall pain or extreme fatigue.

- If the liver is affected, symptoms may include nausea, extreme fatigue, increased abdominal girth, swelling of the feet and hands due to fluid collection and yellowing or itchy skin.

- If the lymph nodes of the belly are affected, it may cause bloating, a swollen belly or loss of appetite.

•If the brain or spinal cord is affected, symptoms may include pain, confusion, memory loss, headache, blurred or double vision, difficulty with speech, difficulty with movement or seizures.

TNM system for colorectal cancer

The most commonly used colorectal cancer staging system is known as the TNM system, which has been established by the American Joint Committee on Cancer. The TNM staging system looks at three key factors to determine the stage of cancer:

•**Tumor (T)** looks at how far the primary tumor has grown into the wall of the colon or rectum, and if it has expanded into nearby areas.

•**Lymph node (N)** examines the extent of the cancer spread to nearby lymph nodes.

•**Metastasis (M)** refers to whether cancer has spread to other parts of the body, such as the liver, lungs or brain.

A number (0-4) or the letter X is assigned to each factor. Using this colorectal cancer staging system, a higher number indicates increasing severity. For instance, a T1 score indicates a smaller tumor than a T2 score. The letter X means the information could not be assessed.

Once the T, N and M scores have been assigned, an overall stage is determined, and thus treatment options can be explored.

Primary tumor (T)

The primary tumor can be categorized as T0 up to T4 for colorectal cancer. Below is a further description of how tumors are defined using the TNM staging system.

TX: The main tumor cannot be assessed.

T0: There is no evidence of a primary tumor.

Tis (carcinoma in situ): In situ means that the cancer is in the earliest stage, and it has not grown beyond the lining of the colon or rectum.

T1: The tumor has grown through the lining (muscularis mucosa) of the colon or rectum.

T2: The tumor has expanded through the second layer of lining (submucosa) of the colon or rectum and into the outer layer (muscularis propria).

T3: The cancer has grown through the muscularis propria and into the outer layers of the colon or rectum, but not all the way through. The cancer has not spread to any nearby organs or tissue.

T4a: The cancer has grown all the way through the wall of the colon or rectum, and has expanded to the surface of nearby organs.

T4b: The cancer has grown through the wall of the colon or rectum and has now affected nearby tissues or organs.

Regional lymph nodes (N)

N0: The cancer has not spread into the lymph nodes.

N1: The cancer has spread to 1 to 3 regional lymph nodes.

N2: The cancer has spread to more than 4 regional lymph nodes.

N2a: Cancerous cells have been located in 4 to 6 regional lymph nodes.

N2b: Cancerous cells have been found in more than 7 lymph nodes.

Distant metastasis (M)

M0: The cancer has not spread to distant organs.

M1: The cancer has spread to distant organs.

M1a: Cancerous cells have spread to one distant organ.

M1b: Cancerous cells have spread to more than one distant organ.

Treatment of colon cancer, by stage

Treatment for colon cancer is based largely on the stage (extent) of the cancer, but other factors can also be important. People with colon cancers that have not spread to distant sites usually have surgery as the main or first treatment. Adjuvant   (additional) chemotherapy may also be used. Most adjuvant treatment is given for about 6 months.

Treating stage 0 colon cancer

Since stage 0 colon cancers have not grown beyond the inner lining of the colon, surgery to take out the cancer is typically all that is needed. This can be done in most cases by removing the polyp (polypectomy) or local excision through a colonoscope. Removing part of the colon (partial colectomy) may occasionally be needed if a tumor is too big to be removed by local excision.

Treating stage I colon cancer

Stage I colon cancers have grown into the layers of the colon wall, but they have not spread outside the colon wall itself (or into the nearby lymph nodes).

Stage I includes cancers that were part of a polyp. If the polyp is removed completely during colonoscopy, with no cancer cells at the edges (margins) of the removed sample, no other treatment may be needed. If the cancer in the polyp is high grade cancer cells at the edges of the polyp, more surgery may be advised. You may also be advised to have more surgery if the polyp couldn't be removed completely or if it had to be removed in many pieces, making it hard to see if cancer cells were at the edges. For cancers not in a polyp, partial colectomy - surgery to remove the section of colon that has cancer and nearby lymph nodes - is the standard treatment. You typically will not need any additional treatment.

Treating stage II colon cancer

Many stage II colon cancers have grown through the wall of the colon, and possibly into nearby tissue, but they have not yet spread to the lymph nodes. Surgery to remove the section of the colon containing the cancer along with nearby lymph nodes (partial colectomy) may be the only treatment needed. But your doctor may recommend adjuvant chemotherapy (chemo after surgery) if your cancer has a higher risk of coming back (recurring) because of certain factors, such as:

•The cancer looks very abnormal (is high grade) when viewed under a microscope.

•The cancer has grown into nearby blood or lymph vessels.

•The surgeon did not remove at least 12 lymph nodes.

•Cancer was found in or near the margin (edge) of the surgical specimen, meaning that some cancer may have been left behind.

•The cancer had blocked off (obstructed) the colon.

•The cancer caused a perforation (hole) in the wall of the colon.

Not all doctors agree on when chemo should be used for stage II colon cancers. It's important for you to discuss the pros and cons of chemo with your doctor, including how much it might reduce your risk of recurrence and what the likely side effects will be. If chemo is used, the main options include 5-FU and leucovorin, or capecitabine, but other combinations may also be used. If your surgeon is not sure all of the cancer was removed because it was growing into other tissues, he or she may advise radiation therapy to try to kill any remaining cancer cells in the area of your abdomen where the cancer was growing.

Treating stage III colon cancer

Stage III colon cancers have spread to nearby lymph nodes, but they have not yet spread to other parts of the body. Surgery to remove the section of the colon with the cancer along with nearby lymph nodes (partial colectomy) followed by adjuvant chemo is the standard treatment for this stage. For chemo, either the FOLFOX (5-FU, leucovorin, and oxaliplatin) or CapeOx (capecitabine and oxaliplatin) regimens are used most often, but some patients may get 5-FU with leucovorin or capecitabine alone based on their age and health needs. Your doctors may also advise radiation therapy if your surgeon thinks some cancer cells might have been left behind after surgery.

Radiation therapy and/or chemo may be options for people who aren't healthy enough for surgery.

Treating stage IV colon cancer

Stage IV colon cancers have spread from the colon to distant organs and tissues. Colon cancer most often spreads to the liver, but it can also spread to other places such as the lungs, peritoneum (the lining of the abdominal cavity), or to distant lymph nodes.

In most cases surgery is unlikely to cure these cancers. However, if there are only a few small areas of cancer spread (metastases) in the liver or lungs and they can be removed along with the colon cancer, surgery may help you live longer and may even cure you. This would mean having a partial colectomy to remove the section of the colon containing the cancer along with nearby lymph nodes, plus surgery to remove the areas of cancer spread. Chemo is typically given as well, before and/or after surgery. In some cases, hepatic artery infusion may be used if the cancer has spread to the liver.

If the metastases cannot be removed because they are too large or there are too many of them, chemo may be given before any surgery (neoadjuvant chemo). Then, if the tumors shrink, surgery to remove them may be tried. Chemo would then be given again after surgery. For tumors in the liver, another option may be to destroy them with ablation or embolization.

If the cancer has spread too much to try to cure it with surgery, chemo is the main treatment. Surgery might still be needed if the cancer is blocking the colon (or is likely to do so). Sometimes, such surgery can be avoided by inserting a stent (a hollow metal or plastic tube) into the colon during a colonoscopy to keep it open. Otherwise, operations such as a colectomy or diverting colostomy (cutting the colon above the level of the cancer and attaching the end to an opening in the skin on the abdomen to allow waste out) may be used.

If you have stage IV cancer and your doctor recommends surgery, it's very important to understand the goal of the surgery — whether it is to try to cure the cancer or to prevent or relieve symptoms of the disease.

Most patients with stage IV cancer will get chemo and/or targeted therapies to control the cancer. Some of the most commonly used regimens include:

- FOLFOX: leucovorin, 5-FU, and oxaliplatin (Eloxatin)

- FOLFIRI: leucovorin, 5-FU, and irinotecan (Camptosar)

- CapeOX: capecitabine (Xeloda) and oxaliplatin

- FOLFOXIRI: leucovorin, 5-FU, oxaliplatin, and irinotecan

- One of the above combinations plus either a drug that targets VEGF (bevacizumab [Avastin], ziv-aflibercept [Zaltrap], or ramucirumab [Cyramza]), or a drug that targets EGFR (cetuximab [Erbitux] or panitumumab [Vectibix])

- 5-FU and leucovorin, with or without a targeted drug

- Capecitabine, with or without a targeted drug

- Irinotecan, with or without a targeted drug

- Cetuximab alone

- Panitumumab alone

- Regorafenib (Stivarga) alone

- Trifluridine and tipiracil (Lonsurf)

The choice of regimens depends on several factors, including any previous treatments you've had and your overall health. If one of these regimens is no longer effective, another may be tried.

Treating recurrent colon cancer

Recurrent cancer means that the cancer has returned after treatment. The recurrence may be local (near the area of the initial tumor), or it may be in distant organs.

Local Recurrence

If the cancer comes back locally, surgery (often followed by chemo) can sometimes help you live longer and may even cure you. If the cancer can't be removed surgically, chemo may be tried first. If it shrinks the tumor enough, surgery may be an option. This would again be followed by more chemo.

Distant recurrence

If the cancer comes back in a distant site, it is most likely to appear first in the liver. Surgery may be an option for some patients. If not, chemo may be tried first to shrink the tumor(s), which may then be followed by surgery to remove them. Ablation or embolization techniques might also be an option to treat some liver tumors.

If the cancer has spread too much to be treated with surgery, chemo and/or targeted therapies may be used. Possible regimens are the same as for stage IV disease. Your options depend on which, if any, drugs you received before the cancer came back and how long ago you received them, as well as on your health. You may still need surgery at some point to relieve or prevent blockage of the colon or other local complications. Radiation therapy may be an option to relieve symptoms as well.

REFERENCES

1   http://www.lungcancer.org/

2   http://www.cancer.ie/

3   http://www.mdanderson.org/

4   http://www.webmd.com/cancer/stomach-gastric-cancer

5   Augustin HG (1998) Antiangiogenic tumour therapy: will it work?Trends in Pharmacological Sciences 19: 216–222.

6   Meyer T and Hart IR (1998) Mechanisms of tumour metastasis. European Journal of Cancer 34: 214–221

7   Sikora K (1999) Developing a global strategy for cancer. European Journal of Cancer 35: 24–31

8   http://www.nlm.nih.gov/medlineplus/cancergeneral.html

9   http://www.cancernet.nci.nih.gov/

10   National Cancer Institute. Lasers in Cancer Treatment. Accessed at www.cancer.gov/cancertopics/factsheet/Therapy/lasers on July 25,

2013.

11   www.cancer.gov

12   www.facs.org

13   Gamboa-Vignolle C,Ferrari-Carballo T, Arrieta O, et al. (2012)Whole-brain irradiation with concomitant daily fixed-dose Temozolomide for brain metastases treatment: A randomised phase II trial. Radiotherapy and Oncology: doi:10.1016/j.radonc.2011.12.004

14   Kondziolka, D., Kalkanis, S. N., Mehta, M. P., Ahluwalia, M., & Loeffler, J. S. (2014). It is time to reevaluate the management of patients with brain metastases. Neurosurgery, 75(1), 1-9.

15   Ramakrishna, N., Temin, S., Chandarlapaty, S., Crews, J. R., Davidson, N. E., Esteva, F. J. & Lin, N. U. (2014). Recommendations on disease management for patients with advanced human epidermal growth factor receptor 2–positive breast cancer and brain metastases: American Society of Clinical Oncology clinical practice

guideline. Journal of Clinical Oncology, 32(19), 2100-2108

16   www.els.net

17   Guidance for Comprehensive Cancer Control Planning, vol. 1: Guidelines, Division of Cancer Prevention and Control, Centers for Disease Control and Prevention, 4770 Buford Highway, NE, Atlanta, GA 30341, 25 March 2002, p. 122.

Online version:

http://www.cdc.gov/cancer/ncccp/cccpdf/Guidance-Guidelines .pdf (accessed 18 September 2006).

18   http://www4.dr-rath-foundation.org/pdf-files/cancer_book.pdf

19   http://www.cancer.org/

20   https://www.iarc.fr

21   http://www.cancercenter.com/cancer/

22   http://icmr.nic.in/cancer.pdf

23   Lippitz, B., Lindquist, C., Paddick, I., Peterson, D., O'Neill, K., &

Beaney, R. (2014). Stereotactic radiosurgery in the treatment of brain metastases: the current evidence. Cancer Treatment Reviews, 40(1), 48-59

24   Nayak, L., Lee, E. Q., & Wen, P. Y. (2012). Epidemiology of brain metastases. Current Oncology Reports, 14(1), 48-54.

25   Saad, S., Wang, T. J., Jani, A., Qureshi, Y. H., Yaeh, A., Nanda, T., & Isaacson, S. R. (2014). BM29: Number of Brain Metastases Influences Survival Following Gamma Knife Radiosurgery. Neuro-Oncology, 16(suppl 5), v38-v38.

26   http://www.who.int/

27   Wegner, R. E., Leeman, J. E., Kabolizadeh, P., Rwigema, J. C., Mintz, A. H., Burton, S. A., & Heron, D. E. (2015). Fractionated stereotactic radiosurgery for large brain metastases. American Journal of Clinical Oncology, 38(2), 135-139.

28   Sahgal, A., Aoyama, H., Kocher, M., Neupane, B., Collette, S., Tago,

M. & Chang, E. L. (2015). Phase 3 trials of stereotactic radiosurgery with or without whole-brain radiation therapy for 1 to 4 brain metastases: individual patient data meta-analysis. International Journal of Radiation Oncology, Biology, and Physics, 91(4), 710-717.

29   Gazit, I., Har-Nof, S., Cohen, Z. R., Zibly, Z., Nissim, U., & Spiegelmann, R. (2015). Radiosurgery for brain metastases and cerebral edema. Journal of Clinical Neuroscience: Official Journal of the Neurosurgical Society of Australasia, 22(3), 535-538.

30   Wong, E., Tsao, M., Zhang, L., Danjoux, C., Barnes, E., Pulenzas, N. & Chow, E. (2015). Survival of patients with multiple brain metastases treated with whole-brain radiotherapy. CNS Oncology, 4(4), 213-224.